MW01284851

Dedicated in memory of

PRESTON BLUE

written by Ihkand Mason

illustrated by FunkGraphicZ

It's Saturday morning, Ihzick and Smacky wake up to eat breakfast and watch cartoons.

Ihzick says: “Wanna go downstairs and play some music?"

“Sure let's go!" says Smacky

”...but not until I finish my pancakes....YUM!!" says Ihzick while stuffing his face.

The brothers go to the basement where their dad has a studio and lots of musical equipment, like drums, keyboards, a bass guitar and some congas.

Smacky plays congas and Ihzick plays the drums. They begin to create many different percussion beats.

The brothers answer the door and sure enough, Darnell, Melvin and Kelvin (the twins from down the street) are waiting on the front porch.

"WHAT'S UP GUYS!!" Ihzick says with excitement.

"Nothing, what were y'all doing?" says Darnell.

"We were practicing." says Ihzick.

"Coooooooool, we just...." Darnell quickly stops!

Everyone pauses and says "WHAT'S THAT SOUND?"

"What sound?" says Melvin.

"That sound!!" Smacky yells.

Everyone starts looking around to find out where it is...

Once the show was over, they all ran back to Ihzick and Smacky's house.

Each one still amazed and excited to see if they can play what they just heard.

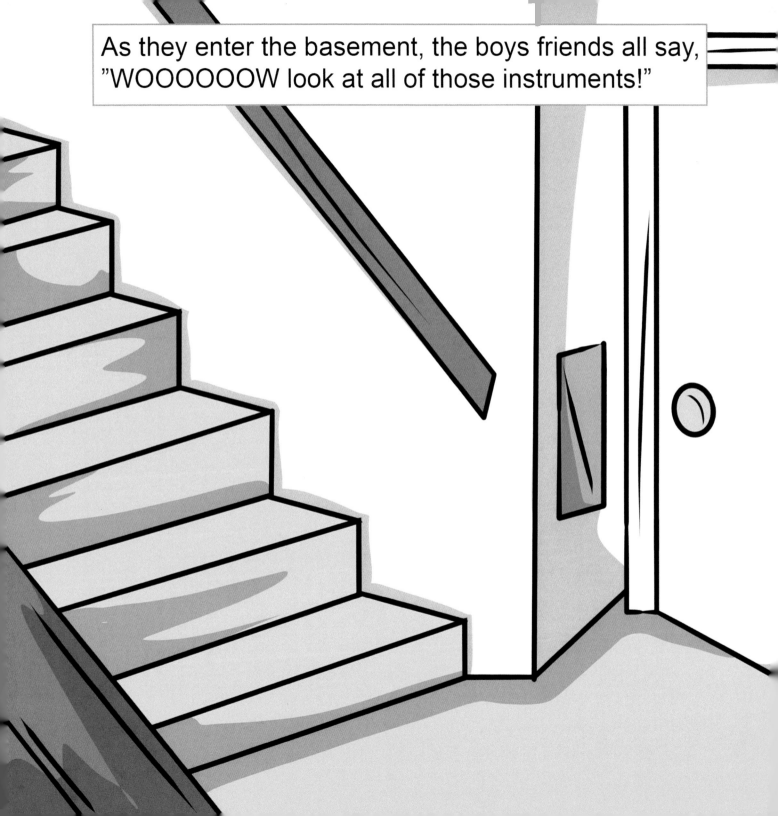

Darnell grabbed the bass guitar. He loves the low deep sound it makes when you slide and pluck on the strings..... "Vaaarooooooooom"

Melvin and Kelvin had taken piano classes in school before, so they ran straight to the keyboards.

Kelvin likes to play Hip Hop and Rhythm & Blues (R&B)

Melvin likes to play Jazz and Classical music

Ihzick loves the drums because his dad plays them also. He likes to hit the cymbals hard, kick the bass drum and bang on the snare....

"BOOM SLAPBOOM BOOM SLAP BOOMBOOM"

Smacky went back to the congas. He loves to play them because you beat them with your hands....
"BAP BOO BAP BOOBOO BAP BOO BAP BOO"

Together they played for hours and hours, trying over and over to duplicate what they just heard because this was.....

THE DAY THEY FOUND...GO-GO!

Go-Go:

continuous, heavy rhythmic patterns performed on multiple congas, timbale and roto-toms, along with tambourine and cowbell parts, while driven by heavy-footed drumming and punctuated by the audiences "call-and-response" as in many African-American church sermons.

for more information
www.whatsgogo.com

Special thank you to
Sherita, Ihmond, Ihyana, Ihnaya and Ihkeem
for encouraging me to continue to crank!!

Made in the USA
Middletown, DE
23 August 2023

36732478R00020